Heart of the Mystic

Contemplations of Mystical Wisdom

Heart of the Mystic

Contemplations of Mystical Wisdom

Jerry Thomas

MYSTICAL HEART PRESS

Heart of the Mystic: Contemplations of Mystical Wisdom

ISBN 1-59457-994-6

Library of Congress Control Number: 2003105016

Published by StillPoint Retreats
117 Walnut Hill Rd.
Derry, NH 03038
www.stillpointretreats.com

Printed in the United States of America

Dedicated to Padre Pio
an embodiment of Love Itself

Contents

Introduction

The Heart of the Mystic is a collection of the sayings and summations of many of the great God-Realized Teachers. Many of these quotes and summaries were used to illustrate certain points in two previous books of mine describing the ageless mystical path and its perspective of unity, love, and peace: Body of Time, Soul of Eternity and State of Grace.

Each concept is in itself a meditation of wisdom. In Mystical Spirituality, wisdom is defined simply and elegantly as **"the ability to see the finite through the eyes of the Infinite."**

I recommend that you first scan the book cover to cover to get a sense of the content. Then go back to the beginning and start to read slowly and quietly. When you come upon an idea that strikes you in some way—stop! Put the book down and think about what you have just read. Repeat the words or concept several times to yourself to get the "feel" of it. Then, bring the essence of the words down through the spiritual centers of your body so that the scriptural wisdom can impregnate your very being at a most fundamental level. This is in some ways similar to the ancient Christian monastic practice of Lexio Divina— making Divine Wisdom active in the transformation of the human intellect, nourishing the Soul within, and bringing us to the goal of life, Divine Union.

In this practice I suggest that you start with an awareness at the area of the crown of your head. Imagine the idea or words residing at that spot. Repeat the scriptural phrase several times until you are comfortable with its inner sound and cadence. Then do the same with an area at the point between your eyebrows. Repeat the phrase several times. Let it "sink in." Feel it permeating that area like a warm light. Rest the idea there, then move to the area of the throat. Do the same there as you did at the point between the eyebrows. Now move to the area of your heart, or the point in the center of the chest. Repeat the idea to yourself many times over until you naturally stop. Allow yourself to drift off into the silent space where this contemplation brings you.

Contemplation is the process of allowing scripture to become alive in your consciousness

Use this procedure daily with a scriptural meditation that appeals to you until you have a sense that its essence has taken root deep within you. Take days, weeks, or months—it doesn't matter. One small fragment of scripture, when taken to its source, can provide great, great understanding, a profound shift in perspective, spiritual wisdom, and removal of suffering due to ignorance of God and our True Self. Only then, when you are ready, move on to find something else that you resonate with.

Often people will find one particular scriptural quote and make it a lifelong contemplation and spiritual friend. For almost forty years *"Seek first the Kingdom of Heaven, and all else shall be added unto you"* has been the cornerstone of my contemplative life. I never get tired of it, or the place that it takes me, or the effect it has had on my life, or the continuously new meanings and understandings it brings to me. It has become the polestar of priority and the guiding light of discrimination between what is truly important and what can get me sidetracked on my spiritual journey.

Knowing God

The mind (logic and reason) cannot investigate, experience, and know that which is beyond itself.

God reveals Himself through the heart (the core of one's being). God cannot be known by reading, theorizing, or thinking.

There are essentially three ways of knowing:

1. **Knowing via the Senses** (Empirical Knowledge): Through the experiences of the senses, knowledge is taken in and assimilated. Here one attempts to experience God (the Essence) through His forms. What is experienced, in fact, is the "form" aspect of God but

not the full nature of God. We see a partial reflection of God in His creation.

2. **Knowing via the Mind** (Logical Knowledge): Using reason and theory, we attempt to come up with a notion of a First Cause, a Supreme Being, an idea of God. However, the nature of God transcends any concepts of which the human mind can possibly conceive. Using the mind, we are as waves on the ocean, attempting to understand the essence and true nature of the ocean by analyzing the surface patterns of the other waves. This only produces endless theories, purposes, meanings, and causalities which lead to a multiplicity of dogmatic religions.

3. **Knowing via Transcendent Intuition** (Mystical Experience): Through spiritual practices that purify the core (heart) of the human being, we are led to the direct experience of God as the human being's natural state. Man is the capacity for God. Mystical "spiritual practices" purify the separate sense of self (ego) and bring the Soul into complete and permanent communion with God. Two primary means of ego purification are, (1) focusing the attention inwards on the inner states of God-Realization, and, (2) practicing discrimination, which is the ability to continuously discern whether an action, thought, word, or deed is, in fact, bringing us closer to our goal of Mystical Union or leading us to distraction with the world of forms.

Do we choose the toys or the Toymaker?

True religion, the process of being led back to God, is sustained not by teaching alone, but by mystical experiences. Religion today often fails because it is perpetuated by people who can only describe the "menu," without the spiritual experience or state of consciousness of the "meal." Over time, mainstream Christianity has gone from being a LIVING REALITY to a set of social and moral principles.

Religious fundamentalism confuses letter for Truth.

Theology tries to use the human mind to understand and describe that which transcends the mind.

Theological scholars expect to find the impossible—a historically accurate account of events of ancient times. They don't take into account that the events were written from many perspectives, from many different states of consciousness and their subsequent different understandings, and from different cultural references and different religious backgrounds over vast periods of time. Is it then surprising that they always find some level of seeming inaccuracy or contradiction? Modern forensic science has clearly demonstrated that two different people viewing the exact same situation will describe two very different sets of events. Now add time, different states of consciousness, different cultures and languages, and we have the confusion and conflict about Living Truth that is rampant in Christianity and other religions today.

A person who imbibes the scriptural works partakes of the Divine Grace that inspired them! Spiritual texts embody the vibration of their authors. Reading texts such as the Bible, the

Bhagavad-Gita, or the works of the great saints and Avatars who dwell in God Consciousness activates the Living Truth within us and coaxes it into our conscious awareness. A partial list of these great saints includes:

> Anandamayi Ma
> Annasuyi Devi
> Buddha
> Jesus
> John of the Cross
> Lawrence of the Resurrection
> Paramahansa Yogananda
> Ramakrishna
> Theresa of Avila

Many people who have just once read the great modern day spiritual classic *Autobiography Of A Yogi*[1], have testified to a profound change in their heart, the core of their being. And that is the point of scripture—scripture being the state of God Consciousness in word form with the distinct ability to impart the quality of that state. We draw the essence of consciousness of that upon which we dwell.

Any concept of scripture, when deeply contemplated and lived fully, can bring one to God Consciousness through its subtle spiritual vibration. Consider just one small aspect of the Christian scriptures such as: "Seek first the Kingdom of Heaven within and all else will come unto you."[2] Without the necessity of reading the Bible cover to cover, the pure understanding of this one teaching is enough to bring one to the full awareness of the Divinity within.

Each aspect of pure scripture is, in itself, a "portal" to Infinite Bliss Consciousness. If a castle has a thousand doors, it is only necessary to enter by one. However, the mind insists on exploring the history, fabric, builder, frame, and efficacy of as many doors as it can survey instead of simply "going through the door." The mind often takes great pride in being a perpetual "seeker," shunning the notion of being a "finder." (Karma?)

By focusing on a Truth, which is "wrapped up" in the word presentation of scripture, you attune to the Divine Energy that is the very Source of inspiration (Divine Consciousness) that led to the writing of the verses.[3]

The secrets of God cannot be unlocked by pure reason but by the discrimination, sweetness, and nobility of a purified heart.

If all of the scriptures were lost,
they could be instantly rewritten,
because they are stored deep
in the hearts of saints

They are stored deep within
our most silent consciousness

The primary domain of True Religion is the direct experience of the "Ground of Being" or the Absolute Divine Principle, the Essence, which is the source and foundation of creation. What we have commonly practiced today is religion that addresses the "Field of Action"—the moral, social, and intellectual aspects of creation's forms. It all comes down to "Essence" and "Form"…what is the focus? True religion, as life, is a mystery (beyond the mind) to be lived from the heart (core), and not a problem to be solved (by the fundamentalist or theological mind).

The essence of Christianity
is direct communion with God,
a realization of the reality of God within

Without that, we are stuck in a world
of inadequate intellectualism

One simple example serves to illustrate this richness of the depth of Christ's teachings and how some of it seems lost is in contemporary Christianity. Christ gave many messages, but there are three primary messages He gave to everyone. However, each person heard one more prominently than the others because that one was most appropriate and productive for that person's state of consciousness and growth at that time.

Christ's primary message to the masses was to love one another and keep the commandments.

To the more spiritually hungry, He told them that what they are looking for is the *"Kingdom of Heaven, which is within."* [4]

And to His nearest disciples He gave the mystical message of the Sermon on the Mount. More specifically, He encouraged them to strive for greater states of God Consciousness when He told them *"I and the Father are One."*[5] And that, in fact, the Will of the Father is that we should become perfect (complete) as the Father in Heaven is Perfect. In other words, He said that God's Will is that we merge into the Supreme State of Ultimate Reality, the abode of the Unmanifest "Father," knowing ourselves as pure Spirit. Until then, and along the way, love one another, and seek the Peace, Joy, and Wisdom of the Inner Self, the Kingdom of Heaven within.

This book ends as it begins, with the One Great Mystical Spiritual Truth:

There is only One Consciousness
There is only One Doer
And It is All Perfect!

And at the very end is *"The Bigger, Bigger Picture"* which is Divine Love's celebration of heroic humanity's courage to take on the most difficult mission of all possible missions—that of a human incarnation on this earth plane.

Love and Great Peace,
Jerry Thomas
Derry, New Hampshire
April 2003

[Note: Parts of this Introduction were excerpted from my book *Body of Time, Soul of Eternity*]

About
Scriptural Reading

Scripture is consciousness in the form of thought
communicated through word symbols

In scripture, words are used to try to describe the Unbounded Presence and Truth within our bounded and limited reality. A primary function of reading sacred scripture is that it helps to eliminate ignorance and misconception, and somewhat "rewires" the finite human mind to receive Eternal Truth.

As the outer forms of scripture seem to be moralistic and literal when read from the state of normal waking consciousness, the inner meaning of scripture is, in fact, pure consciousness. These words are expressed in limited form and their real meaning can only be known from the inner state of the Soul, the state of Silence, the State of Grace. These word forms are not Truth in themselves, but they point to Truth. They are not the actual stars in the heavens, but the signs that point the way. Reading scripture from the state of Silence (the meditative state of inner peace) allows us to go to the source consciousness from which the scriptures were written.

For example, an academic theologian who knows only the meaning of the words but has not experienced the spirit from which they have come, is apt to have a very different understanding of the message of a great master, such as Christ, than one who is God Realized and in the state of Christ Consciousness himself.

Our state of consciousness dictates the level and the amount of scripture that we can understand

The inner meaning of the scriptures is what brings about changes in people's hearts. Our understanding of them is like a personal measure of our spiritual attainment. To look only at the meaning of the words is to obfuscate the true meaning of the Essence that they are trying to convey. Here, we can mistake form for Essence. Literalism is the death of Spirit.

Through spiritual practices that purify the core (heart) of the human being, the direct experience of God is the human being's natural state. Man is the capacity for God. These simple mystical "spiritual practices," such as contemplation of sacred scripture, are a means to purify the separate sense of self (ego) and bring the soul into complete and permanent communion with God. The primary means of ego purification is the practice of discrimination—or, the ability to continuously discern whether an action, thought, word, or deed is, in fact, bringing us closer to our goal of Mystical Union or leading us to distraction with the world of forms. Do we choose the toys or the Toymaker? Mystical Contemplation nurtures and strengthens our ability to make good judgments based on keen discrimination.

We read scripture to superimpose
Truth on the incomplete understanding
found in relative knowledge

The stories and writings of saints are impregnated with their consciousness and can lead us to clearer understanding of our true nature and to states of inner Peace and Bliss. Once made part of our being, they become vehicles of Self Realization.

The words of the great
God-realized Beings are
vibratory wisdom from their Consciousness
waiting to be transmitted to
the humble mind,
the pure and yearning heart,
the selfless Soul

The Heart of the Mystic draws from the wisdom of the Old and New Testaments of the Bible, the Bhagavad-Gita, the Koran, the writings of the Sufi saints, the Buddha, western and eastern mystics, John of the Cross, Theresa of Avila, Ramakrishna, Yogananda, Shirdi Sai Baba, Anandamayi Ma and many, many others. Mystical words and teachings, although spoken differently, all refer back to the central Truth that there is only One Consciousness—One God. All of creation has come from that One Source and **it is the destiny of all creation to return back to its Source!**

Scriptural Readings

We can live our lives for ourselves

Or live our lives

So that God can live through us.

Love is a fire in the heart

that burns up

All but the Beloved's wishes

The source of all suffering

Is the sense of separation

From our Inner Self

Grace is the capacity

To take Life with ease

The Ultimate experience of
self-acceptance

Is the result of Wholeness -

Union with the Inner Self

You give until there is nothing left.
And when there is nothing left –
There is God.

There is only
One Consciousness
One Doer
and it is all Perfect

Nothing short of the direct experience of God
will ever satisfy our
need for wholeness, fulfillment, and completion

Man is the capacity for God

The Human Being returning to God
is the pinnacle of Creation

The One becomes many;
the many differentiate
and return to the One

God is Essence,
the all-pervading Silence

Creation is Form,
a vibration on the surface of Silence

Unbounded Essence can contain
limited form

but limited form
cannot contain Unbounded Essence

The Ocean can contain the wave
The wave cannot contain the Ocean

The destiny of the Soul
is to know and become one
with the absolute fullness of
Ultimate Reality

The only constant in creation is change
The greatest delusion is that we can control it

"Delusion is not feeling
that He alone performs every action"[6]

Although Consciousness takes many forms

Ultimately there is only
One Consciousness
One Doer
and it is all Perfect

and that is the Truth of Ultimate Reality

The Soul is an individualized
aspect of God

Ego is a state of the soul forgetting its nature
and identifying with the organs of experience —
body, mind, and senses

A successful life is not measured
by what we do
but by the Realization
of who we are

Consciousness is the degree to which
Essence is reflected in form
"For what does it profit a man
if he gains (or saves) the world
and loses his soul?"[7]

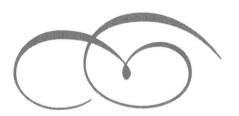

Our primary fear is the fear of loss –
objects, feelings, people, and relationships
All those things we can never fully possess

Our primary grief is for the loss of
that which seeks to possess us – God

Our primary illusion is in
settling for the toys
instead of the Divine Toymaker

Mystical Union transcends
the ego's frantic desire to create
and find fulfillment
in a separate personal reality

"The Kingdom of Heaven is within."[8]

"Seek first the Kingdom of Heaven
and all else shall be added unto you."[9]

Spirituality is directional in nature,

a moving towards the Inner Self –

and God

The one goal of spirituality
is our merging with God
and living beyond the dream of duality

It is "Being in the world, but not of it."

We can spend this lifetime getting

to know ourselves

or getting to know God

The source of all suffering and karma
is the separation from our Inner Self

The nature of the Soul is
Love, Peace, Wisdom, and Joy

Truth is perceived differently
in different states of consciousness

The plan for creation is for the Unlimited
to experience Its Infinite Unboundedness
within the boundaries of the finite

The desire to love God
is the fulfillment of all desire

There is only one true Beloved

Silence is the home of God in creation

Silence is the means of
restructuring our consciousness

God has everything but our love

Love is a principle of action,
not a quality of behavior

When we relegate such a
profound principle as Love
to a set of learned behaviors and attitudes,
the magnitude of its depths
and the magnificence of its Divinity
becomes trivialized

"Seek first the Kingdom of Heaven within."[10]

That is the state where Love resides
and from that state you become Love
and Love's perfect instrument of expression

To truly love
is to adopt the state of Inner Silence
and act from there

The state of Grace is the state of the Soul

It is the home of Love, Peace, Wisdom, and Joy

Grace is a gift to those who give

their hearts and lives to God

Generally God's Will is "What Is"

The free and open space between

our inevitable karma

is where we can exercise free will

God's Will is simple:

Fulfill your responsibilities
Serve others where you can
Remember Him

God's Will is all-inclusive:

God's Will contains His Will that we can choose

to exert what appears to be our own will

God's Will is absolute:

Ultimately
God is the Sole Doer

Wisdom is seeing the finite
through the Eyes of the Infinite

Wisdom cannot be learned or attained

nor can Love, Joy, and Peace

be learned or attained,

but the state from which these emanate

can be attained

That is the state of the Soul –

the State of Grace

Faith is the mortal eyes seeing
the Divine Hand in the Play of Life

Joy is the effervescent contentment with what is

True Joy is expressed by the happiness
of taking from Life what is given

Suffering is trying to take from Life
what is not given

Know your True Nature

"Be Perfect as the Father in Heaven is Perfect."[11]

"Love is a fire in the heart
that burns up all but the Beloved's wishes."[12]

Love is not an emotion
It is a profound commitment
to an ideal of wholeness
that fulfills our Inner Longing

Meditation is merging with Silence

Mantra is a mystical sound
It is the Name of God ~
the sound of Silence

"I saw My Lord in a dream and I asked
'How am I to find You?'
He replied, 'Leave yourself and come.'"[13]

Prayer is the consent
to God's Presence within us

The spiritual process is about
waking from the dream of Creation
and living beyond duality

The true teacher does not give knowledge alone

The true teacher gives the

experience of God – Ultimate Reality

The great spiritual commandment is

Know God First

(all the rest is mere commentary)

The great spiritual technique is:

Keep your mind on God

God is simple

Everything else is complex

Humility is knowing that God is the sole doer

The human mind can never fathom

Divine Causality

Wisdom is seeing the finite
from the eyes of the infinite

Ignorance is seeing the finite
from the eyes of the finite

The mind can't know that which transcends it

Excitation is the basis of the wave

Silence is the basis of activity

Trust is Faith in action

A sense of personal autonomy
is too high a price to pay
for loss of Divine Union

We look to self-empowerment only to realize
that we are empowering the wrong self

True healing is re-establishing union
with our Inner Self

It is moving from the ego state of separation
to the state of wholeness ~
the State of Grace

Most often what we are experiencing now

is the result of forces set into play

many, many lifetimes ago

The primal disease
and the source of all human suffering
is ignorance of our True Nature

True healing does not mean a temporal cure
but an elevation to Wholeness or
Higher States of Consciousness

It doesn't matter so much what happens to us
as what we become through what happens to us

Divine Perfection is reflected in perfect
Love, Peace, Wisdom, and Joy
and not necessarily reflected
in an ideal of a perfect body
or an ideal society

Creation is God's Play

The One becomes the many
and the many go back to the One

Spiritual evolution is not evolution
of the species, or evolution of forms,
or the evolution of that which is in duality

It is going beyond duality
It is the ascent of man to God
It is form returning back to Essence

Excitation characterizes the ego state

Silence characterizes the soul state

Ecstasy characterizes the state
of God Communion

The human being "going forth"
is the wonder of creation

The human being "being all it can be"
is the fulfillment of creation

The human being "returning to God"
is the pinnacle of creation

Until we reach beyond the ego state
we experience suffering, which is the
natural consequence of the separation
from God and our Inner Self

Creation is an act of repulsion

from the Source

the descent of Spirit into matter

Spiritual Evolution is a reversal

of the Creation process,

transcending matter

and returning to Source

Energy and light are subtle forms –
the substance of duality
commonly mistaken for
Ultimate Reality

God is not energy, light, or sound
Creation is energy, light, and sound

As the ocean is the source
and the wave the manifestation

God is the Source,
Light and energy are the manifestation

As separation from the Inner Self
is the primary stress of human existence,
the primary pain of human existence is
putting our individual will
before God's Will

Karma is a balancing and purification
of certain tensions that have
overshadowed our state of inner equanimity

Control is fear in action

The ego is fundamentally innocent
yet feels great responsibility for its state
and the state of things in general

Although disguised in desires
for things of the world,
the driving desire of all mankind
is to reunite with its Source

There is no perfection in the relative

Often God will use a thorn to remove a thorn

and suffering to remove suffering

We are loved by Love Itself
and everything that is happening is out of
His Infinite Love for us

What we focus on we become

In the State of Grace,

equanimity and peace of mind are untouched

by the crashing waves of karma

Spiritual practice is refocusing the mind

and drawing it to its Source

Prayer is the consent to
God's Presence within us –
and the receptivity to
God working within us

There is only

One Consciousness
One Doer
and it is all Perfect

Silence vibrating is Creation
Silence flowing is Love
Silence shared is Friendship

Silence seen is Infinity
Silence heard is the Name of God
Silence expressed is Beauty

Silence maintained is Strength

Silence omitted is Suffering

Silence experienced is Peace

Silence recorded is Sacred Scripture
Silence preserved is the Mystical Path
Silence given is Grace

Silence received is Joy

Silence perceived is Wisdom

Silence stabilized is Realization

Silence alone Is

There is only
One Consciousness
One Doer
and it is all Perfect

The Bigger, Bigger Picture

For a minute, let's let go of the small stuff and see it all from a bigger picture.

Let's "make believe" that just before creation occurred God brought all the Souls together, all those who were to go out through the various universes and planes to experience His creation for Him. Remember that the purpose of it all was for the Creator to experience the completeness of His Existence. He who is Unlimited has not experienced limitation and needs to have this experience in order to completely differentiate and be complete.

So, here we are, all gathered together and we are getting our assignments. And then God says, "I need some volunteers for the most difficult of all assignments. I need Souls to go to the earth plane to experience the worst of all possible conditions that I can imagine for Myself to experience. I will send you to a plane where you will become enchanted with the manifestations of light, sound, thought, and matter. It is a very dense plane. It is the densest in all of creation. It is also the one of greatest suffering, for you will forget your true nature, forget

Me, and suffer greatly from the separation, loneliness, depression, disappointment, illness, and anxiety of trying to find Me and all of My gifts outside of yourself. You will have to endure many, many lifetimes. You will be deceived by false prophets and teachers who will promise you My Heaven on this earth. Your beautiful Soul nature will be covered with an ignorance— a state of ego consciousness, the false pseudo-soul. Worst of all, you will think I have forgotten you and don't love you. These conditions sadden Me greatly, but it is necessary that I achieve the nearly impossible on this earth plane, the most difficult and paradoxical of all experiences.

"I must fulfill the goal of my creation."

"I must experience My Unboundedness within boundaries. I must forget that I am One and think I am many. And when this has occurred, I must reverse the process of creation and find Myself again.

"Who loves me enough to accept this impossible and painful assignment? Who loves Me enough to endure and allow for My completion?"

And then a number of great hero Souls shouted out in unison "We, Lord! We, Lord. We love You and only You and we will show you the depth of our love by overcoming all obstacles that you place in our path. Send us!"

At that moment the human race was born
and God knew that He was loved beyond measure

And here we are, struggling and being human, trying to remember that we are God experiencing His creation through us.

From this perspective it is easier to be more compassionate with yourself and others...look around at the other hero Souls (no matter what state they are in) who have also volunteered to undergo the earth plane to fulfill the mission of creation. We are loved dearly by Love Itself...and when we reach our Home there will be joy and celebration without end!

"Seek First the Kingdom of Heaven
which is within,
then all else shall be added unto you."[15]

Recommended Reading

1. Anandamayi Ma, *As the Flower Sheds Its Fragrance*, Calcutta, India: Shree Shree Anandamayee Charitable Society (Available through the Blue Dove Foundation, www.bluedove.com, 858-623-3330)

2. Bacovin, Helen, translator, *The Way of a Pilgrim*, New York, NY: Doubleday Press

3. Burrows, Ruth, *Ascent to Love: the Spiritual Teachings of St. John of the Cross*, Denville, NJ: Dimension Books

4. Conway, Timothy, *Women of Power and Grace*, Santa Barbara, CA: Wake-Up Press

5. Dabholkal, Govind, translated by Nagest Vasudev Gunaji, *Shri Sai Satcharita, The Wonderful Life and Teachings of Shri Sai Baba*, Mumbai, India: Shri Sai Baba Sansthan. Call StillPoint Communications (603-434-2264) to order.

6. Keating, Thomas, *Invitation to Love*, Amity, NY: Amity House

7. Lawrence, Brother, translated by Robert J. Edmonson, *The Practice of the Presence of God*, Brewster, MA: Paraclete Press

8. Markides, Kyriacos, *The Mountain of Silence: A Search for Orthodox Spirituality*, New York, NY: Doubleday Press

9. Paramahansa Yogananda, *Autobiography of a Yogi*, Los Angeles, CA: Self-Realization Fellowship

10. Paramahansa Yogananda, *God Talks with Arjuna: The Bhagavad Gita*, Los Angeles, CA: Self-Realization Fellowship

11. Paramahansa Yogananda, *The Second Coming of Christ*, Dallas, TX: Amrita Foundation, Inc.

12. Prabhavananda, Swami, *The Sermon on the Mount According to Vedanta*, Hollywood, CA: Vedanta Society

13. Thomas, Jerry, *Body of Time, Soul of Eternity: Mystical Spirituality*, Phoenix, AZ: Mystical Heart Press

14. Thomas, Jerry, *State of Grace: Healing from Within*, call Stillpoint Communication, 603-434-2264, for information

15. Thomas, Jerry, *Fullness of Life: Inner Silence*, call Stillpoint Communication, 603-434-2264, for information

End Notes

1. Paramahansa Yogananda, *Autobiography of a Yogi.*

2. Luke 12:31

3. This process, referred to as "Lexio Divina," is explained in the chapter "About Scriptural Reading."

4. Matthew 6:33

5. John 10:30

6. Annasuya Devi

7. Matthew 16:26

8. Matthew 6:33, Luke 12:31

9. Luke 12:31

10. Luke 12:31

11. Matthew 5:48

12. Sufi saying, author unknown.

13. Sufi saying, author unknown.

14. From the poem "Silence." The author is unknown, but I want to acknowledge the beautiful way in which he/she gave words to the Silence.

15. Luke 12:31

About the Author

Jerry Thomas is an accomplished philosopher, writer, teacher, lecturer, and practitioner of Mystical Spirituality. His broad and diverse education includes extensive study in modern sciences, comparative spirituality, mysticism, and world religions.

He has been a life-long participant and student of both Eastern and Western monastic traditions, with a formal education that includes advanced degrees in science, education, and organizational development.

He is currently the retreat master and founder of the StillPoint Retreats, which is a unique series of experiential seminars and workshops exploring Mystical Spirituality as a concept and an experience. In these silent retreat experiences, he teaches the principles of the mystical tradition as well as simple methods of attaining the fulfillment of the inner, Transcendent Self.

Jerry has two other books available that continue the themes covered in this book: *Body of Time, Soul of Eternity* and *State of Grace*, both available through StillPoint Retreats.

You can contact Jerry Thomas through StillPoint Communications:

117 Walnut Hill Road
Derry, NH 03038, USA
(603) 434-2264
retreats@stillpointretreats.com
www.stillpointretreats.com

Seminars & Retreats

The StillPoint Silent Retreats, conducted by Jerry Thomas, are designed to provide a deep and abiding experience of the Inner Self, the essence and fulfillment of who we truly are. Each retreat is a balance of time-honored spiritual knowledge as taught by the Masters of the Mystical traditions of all world religions, as well as quiet periods of meditative silence. Simple practices are taught to allow the direct experience of the beautiful inner state from which all such spiritual knowledge flows. There are also periods of group and private meditation, contemplation, walks, rest, and individual study.

These retreats are for those who desire a deeper and more sustained relationship to their Inner Divinity as expressed in the experience of joy, wisdom, and profound inner peace. Although each weekend has a different theme, the core knowledge is that of the way of "Mystical Spirituality," with the focus on experiencing deep inner silence.

Retreats are kept small to maximize personal attention for each individual. No more than fifty participants are accepted for each event. These smaller groups are quieter and more focused.

For further information, contact:
StillPoint Retreats, Inc.
117 Walnut Hill Road
Derry, NH 03038, USA
(603) 434-6100
retreats@stillpointretreats.com
www.stillpointretreats.com

Books by Jerry Thomas

Body of Time, Soul of Eternity: Mystical Spirituality

(ISBN 1-59457-992-X) *Body Of Time, Soul of Eternity* answers from a mystical perspective such questions as the purpose of creation and the purpose of life while articulating clearly and concisely the ancient path of the direct experience of God—Divine Realization. This book is a modern reference to ancient wisdom presented in such a way that it can be appreciated by followers of all traditions.

State of Grace: Healing from Within

(available in 2004) State of Grace reveals thattimeless healing and wholeness is the alignment of the inner and outeraspects of life. The full value of life is spiritual fulfillment, a state that fartranscends physical wellness.

Heart of the Mystic: Contemplations of Mystical Wisdom

(ISBN 1-59457-994-6) *Heart of the Mystic* is a series of inspirational, mystical meditations paraphrased from ancient God-Realized Masters. "Scripture is Consciousness in word form."

All books published by StillPoint Retreats, www.stillpointretreats.com

Books available from your local bookstore, online booksellers, or StillPoint Retreats (603) 434-6100